A Warrior of Hope

A Warrior of Hope

Laurie Hampton

All Scripture quotations, unless otherwise indicated, are taken from the Holy Bible, New International Version®, NIV®. Copyright ©1973, 1978, 1984, 2011 by Biblica, Inc.™ Used by permission of Zondervan. All rights reserved worldwide. www.zondervan.com The "NIV" and "New International Version" are trademarks registered in the United States Patent and Trademark Office by Biblica, Inc.™

Scripture quotations marked (NLT) are taken from the Holy Bible, New Living Translation, copyright ©1996, 2004, 2015 by Tyndale House Foundation. Used by permission of Tyndale House Publishers, Inc., Carol Stream, Illinois 60188. All rights reserved.

The Christian Standard Bible. Copyright © 2017 by Holman Bible Publishers. Used by permission. Christian Standard Bible®, and CSB® are federally registered trademarks of Holman Bible Publishers. All rights reserved.

Scripture is taken from the New Century Version®. Copyright © 2005 by Thomas Nelson. Used by permission. All rights reserved.

Cover Design by LSDesign

Edited by Liz Giertz

A Warrior of Hope

Copyright @ 2019 Laurie Hampton

ISBN: 978-0-578-57072-3

Names: Laurie Hampton, author

Title: A Warrior of Hope

All rights reserved. No part of this publication may be reproduced, stored in a retrieval system, or transmitted in any form or by any means – electronic, mechanical, digital, photocopy, recording, or any other – except for brief quotations in printed reviews, without the prior permission of the author.

Contents

1. Pray, Believe, Receive
2. Lead the Way
3. Strength Training
4. Live Inspired
5. God's Not Late
6. Giants of Faith
7. For What It's Worth
8. Live Fiercely
9. He Lifted Me
10. Confessions of a People Pleaser
11. Motivational Mercies
12. The Secret Place
13. Unmovable Hope
14. God is Your Guide
15. Unfading Beauty
16. Rejoice in Suffering
17. Enough
18. Idle Words
19. Don't Be a Fool
20. But God

21. Spirit and Truth
22. The Hard Question
23. A Good Laugh
24. What We Really Need
25. A Song in My Heart
26. Think Before You Speak
27. Good Gifts
28. I Pinky Swear
29. Restored
30. Our Final Hope

Bonus Devotion: A Quiver of Arrows

Acknowledgments

Writing a book is harder than I thought and more rewarding than I could have ever imagined. None of this would have been possible without the love and support of my amazing husband, Richard. Thank you.

I hope I have not embarrassed my two sons too much in this book. I use examples from their lives and our relationship often in my writing. Kyle and Joel, thanks so much for putting up with me and letting me borrow your stories.

To all of my family, thank you for supporting me as a writer. For encouraging me to move forward and not quit, for reading what I write, and for sharing it with others. I love you guys and am grateful for such a loving and caring family.

I am grateful for my editor, Liz Giertz (www.LizGiertz.com), who partnered with me on this book and deserves credit for her beautiful work. I treasured her encouraging words and prayers along the way. Thank you, Liz!

And most of all, I am exceedingly grateful to the Author of my story. Thank you, God, for whispering into my soul the words of this book.

Introduction

May the God of hope fill you with all joy and peace as you trust in him, so that you may overflow with hope by the power of the Holy Spirit. Romans 15:13

I pray this verse will anchor you in the hope we have in Christ Jesus. That you will be filled to overflowing with joy and peace as you read through the following 30 days of devotions anchored in God's provisions and promises.

Do you see a hopeless end or an endless hope? Hope can be hard to come by, and if there is anything, we need more of it is hope. Hope does not come from people, circumstances, or situations. Hope comes from God.

For years I put my trust in man, I looked to the world to fill a hollow ache I had in my soul to be seen, to be noticed and to be loved. I wasted so many years yearning for that sense of belonging and trying to fit into any creases or cracks I found in a broken world. I joined countless groups in search of belonging and acceptance. I permitted others to speak their truths into my life, only to discover their truths were the wrong size for the hole in my heart.

What changed? I finally surrendered all to God. I fell to my knees when the world knocked me down and tried to steal my identity – to take the rest of what I had not squandered on paying for the wrong solutions. In my fall, I looked up, and I found THE hope.

When I let God come into my heart, He filled me to the point of overflowing, with joy and peace. I love God's extravagance. He is not just giving us a little bit of joy and peace; He is giving us ALL the joy and peace there is to offer, holding nothing back.

Each day of this devotional, you will hear personal stories, Scripture passages, and a positive affirmation that will remind you of God's provisions and promises. I pray God will use A Warrior of Hope to remind you of the hope you have in Christ Jesus. I consider it an honor to pray for all my readers, and I will make it a top priority to be praying for you.

May you experience a deeper, richer relationship with Jesus as you become a Warrior of Hope!

Blessings!
Laurie Hampton

1.

Pray, Believe, Receive

Therefore I tell you, whatever you ask for in prayer, believe that you have received it, and it will be yours. Mark 11:24

Have you ever prayed about something and then been surprised to receive it? This is what happened to me recently. I had the church, my family, and my friends pray for chronic pain I had been suffering with for years. The pain went away, and I was perplexed as to what I had done to cause it to stop.

Can I really pray for anything and expect God to give it to me? As we look at this verse in context and as compared to many other passages in the Bible, the answer is no. James 4:3 tells us that if what we ask for only fuels our own passions, we will not receive and 1 John 5:14 qualifies our prayer request to be heard, only if what we ask for is in God's will.

Our prayers are often motivated by our own interests, passions, and desires. When we pray, we should keep God's interest in mind, and when we lead with that, we can believe what we pray for we will receive.

So, why did God answer my prayer when I clearly did not act out of faith, believing I had already received my healing? Because we know God will work everything together for our good. Even though we may have doubts about our specific prayer being answered, we do not need to doubt that God will always give us what is best.

{A Warrior of Hope Gets What She Prays For}

Pray, believe, and receive. What a great promise for us to begin our journey on. Throughout this devotional, we will end each day with a prayer anchored in the will of God. Together we will pray and believe, trusting God will answer by giving us what is best for each of us.

Heavenly Father, teach me how to recognize your interests above my own. I want to be able to pray boldly and believe in what I ask for. Thank you for always giving me what is in my best interest, even when I doubt my request. In Jesus' name. Amen.

2.

Lead the Way

The LORD himself goes before you and will be with you; he will never leave you nor forsake you. Do not be afraid; do not be discouraged.
Deuteronomy 31:8

What are your biggest fears? Sometimes when I know I am going to be in a place where I will have to face a fear, I find a friend to confide in first. If I am really scared, I might ask someone to be with me during the event. What is your first response to fear?

Everybody was going to see the movie. If I didn't go, I would look like a chicken. My parents had told me, no, but after much begging, I convinced them I would not be scared. I can't believe I sat through the whole movie. It was stupid and not realistic, but when you are with a bunch of teenagers, the talk afterward often brings forth more fears than the actual movie.

So, that night when I stayed at my friend's house, it should not have been a surprise that every sound we heard, was a sign "IT" was alive! My friend's dad ended up taking me home in the middle of the night, and I was very grateful to my father for welcoming me home with a hug instead of a lecture.

We have a friend with us every time we are in situations that scare us. Our friend is the Lord, and He always goes before us to clear the way. The Lord wants us to be brave as Warriors of Hope, to be strong and courageous, not to be afraid or discouraged. His promise to us is that He will never leave or forsake us.

{A Warrior of Hope Lets the Lord Lead the Way}

Doesn't it feel better knowing we are never alone on our journeys? Even on the darkest night or the loneliest trip, we have God walking ahead of us to light the way and clear the path. His promises are always true.

Heavenly Father, who goes before me and leads the way, show me how I can step out further in my ministry. When I am afraid and discouraged, I will look for your tracks in the path ahead of me, knowing for certain that you are there leading me into the light of your promises. In Jesus' name. Amen.

3.

Strength Training

He gives strength to the weary and increases the power of the weak. Isaiah 40:29

Being turned down for an opportunity you want is hard. I bet you have experienced the disappointment that comes from being rejected before too. How did you respond?

My son is a very bright child. He is a senior in high school and going through the college application process. However, he is not a very good test taker, and on top of that, he has a learning disability.

Since the third grade, his dream has been to go to a traditional university, live in a dorm, and get a degree in Civil Engineering. He has, to date received rejection letters from all the traditional universities where he has applied. He has a roadblock to maneuver around.

However, he is not giving up on his dream. I love that this kid has a plan; he even has back up plans for the backup plan. He has pushed through tears, frustrations, and disappointments by leaning into the strength of the Lord. The Lord had given him the strength needed when he was weary and ready to quit.

As you read further down to verse 31 in Isaiah, you come

upon another well-known verse, "They will soar on wings like eagles; they will run and not grow weary, they will walk and not be faint." Isaiah is speaking words of comfort to Israel after their release from captivity, and these same words are an encouragement for us as we walk through adversity in our lives.

{A Warrior of Hope Receives Her Strength from the Lord}

Do you believe God wants you to rise above the storms of life and soar on wings like eagles? I hope you can relax and be confident in His purposes for your life and allow Him to do the strength training necessary for you to enjoy optimal health.

Heavenly Father, I want to fly on wings like eagles; I want to run and not be weary. My heart yearns for your strength in times of trouble. Blessed is the Lord who strengthens my soul. Blessed is the Lord, who is the power in my weakness. Lord, thank you for your power and might. In Jesus' name. Amen.

4.

Live Inspired

In the beginning God created the heavens and the earth.... And God saw that it was good. Genesis 1:1,25

What inspired God to create the heavens and the earth? What inspired Him to make the leaves change colors? How was He inspired to create a whole other ecosystem and put it underwater?

A friend recently asked where I get the inspiration for my writing. The first answer to come to mind was, of course, to give credit to God for my inspiration, and rightly so. But as I think about inspiration, it is more than just an occasional good idea that flies down from heaven, into my mind, and onto the paper.

So, where does inspiration come from? Are inspired thoughts just up there hovering around waiting for me to ask for one? Are they withheld from me if I neglect the process of prayer?

Perhaps the inspiration is never-ending, having been created while in my mother's womb. We know God has given each of us unique gifts for the benefit of the Body of Christ. What if He downloaded the inspiration into us along with the gift and we always have full access to it.

1 Timothy 4:14-15 says, "Do not neglect your gift, which was given you through prophecy when the body of elders laid their hands on you. Be diligent in these matters; give yourself wholly to them, so that everyone may see your progress." We can take the advice Paul gave his protege Timothy and pay attention to our gifts. We are to use our gifts, fine-tune our gifts, and immerse ourselves in our gifts, so all may see our progress and others may benefit from them.

{A Warrior of Hope Lives Inspired}

God is in the inspiration that began in us at birth, wove itself into the fiber of our being, was present in every tiny detail of our history and lives within us always. In other words, we live inspired lives with full access to the bounty of His blessings, far and wide.

Heavenly Father, let me not waste my access to your unlimited and unreserved inspiration. I praise you that you have breathed into my very being the inspiration to make a difference in this world. Holy are you God of our creation. May you always see progress in my gifts. In Jesus' name. Amen.

5.
God's Not Late

For the revelation awaits an appointed time: it speaks of the end and will not prove false. Though it lingers wait for it; it will certainly come and will not delay. Habakkuk 2:3

Waiting is hard work. We all want good things in our lives, but it is hard to wait for God's perfect timing. Do you struggle in times of waiting also? What do you do while waiting?

I had planned a Hawaiian vacation with my husband. My bags were packed, not only was the flight booked, but the plane was probably already on the runway. This was a chance of a lifetime; I was going be in Hawaii, seeing the ocean for only the second time in my life. I was ready to eat fresh pineapple and take long walks along the beach. Finally, the timing was just right.

But it was not meant to be. Just hours before we were to leave for the airport, our plans changed. I was to stay home. You see, God had other plans for me that week. Plans for me to be a parent to my kids, plans for me to honor my family, plans for me to forgive and to trust in God's perfect timing. When God directs our paths, He sometimes leads us in ways that don't make sense to us. Sometimes, He makes us wait longer than we'd like, even when we think we have everything planned just right.

Proverbs 3:5-6 says, "Trust in the Lord with all your heart and lean not on your understanding; in all your ways submit to him, and he will make your paths straight." Waiting is an act of trust. I am learning this as I live in the tension of praying for God's will in my life and believing His timing will be perfect even when there is a last-minute change.

{A Warrior of Hope Trusts God's Timing}

God causes everything to happen at the right time. Our job is not to figure out the timing, but to trust in God's perfect timing. What if we stopped trying to manage everything and let God be God?

Heavenly Father, sometimes it is hard to trust your timing. Help me to have patience in my waiting. Even when the timing does not make sense, help me to know you are purposeful in your decisions and your purposes for me are always good. In Jesus' name. Amen.

6.

Giants of Faith

And without faith it is impossible to please God, because anyone who comes to him must believe that he exists and that he rewards those who earnestly seek him. Hebrews 11:6

Is there a difference between believing and having faith? Many people "believe" Jesus walked the earth. According to James 2:19, even the demons believe He exists. Biblical faith, however, goes beyond the acceptance of facts and puts your eternal destiny in the hands of God.

I find it challenging to have faith when I am facing some of life's more challenging times; illness, job loss, relationship problems, and all the other issues that come from living this side of heaven. Wanting complete control over the circumstances, and the outcome is what feels comfortable. Surrendering control to God, and earnestly seeking Him above any of the world's assurances is what pleases God.

Let's look at some of the Giants of Faith from the Bible to see how they chose to seek God and put their lives in His hands. These giants of faith all had different stories and different circumstances. What they had in common, however, was an uncommon, winning faith.

By faith, Able brings God a pleasing offering. By faith,

Enoch was taken from the earth without dying. By faith, Noah built a boat while his contemporaries laughed at him. By faith, Abraham made a home in a foreign land. By faith, Sarah had children at a very old age. By faith, Moses' parents hid him for three months to save his life. By faith, Rahab welcomed spies into her home.

{A Warrior of Hope Has Faith}

Is God calling you to take a step of faith in something today? How will you respond? Be encouraged knowing the Lord is with you and does not call you to that which He has not prepared a way to succeed according to His good plans.

Heavenly Father, make me a giant of the faith. Let me abide in your presence and feast on your words as I become stronger in my faith. Give me opportunities to grow in faith and keep me focused on you as I earnestly seek you. In Jesus' name. Amen.

7.

For What It's Worth

Are not five sparrows sold for two pennies? Yet not one of them is forgotten by God. Indeed, the very hairs of your head are all numbered. Don't be afraid; you are worth more than many sparrows. Luke 12:6-7

How much money is in your bank account? How many friends do you have on Facebook? How much income does your household earn? Is that what you're worth?

I worked as a Bank Teller when I was in college. At the end of our shift, we would count our drawers. Some of the money was crumpled and worn. Sometimes the bills had tears in them. We counted coins, bills, and checks, and in the end, recorded the tally of our drawers.

On one particular day of the week, around 5 p.m., the local meatpacking plant employees poured into the bank to cash and deposit their checks. Unfortunately, the odors involved with meatpacking are not pleasant, so they and their checks stunk! That odor permeated my nostrils and clung to my hands.

But all that smelly money taught me a valuable lesson.

What was that crumpled twenty-dollar bill or the torn five-dollar bill worth? What was the three-hundred-dollar stinky check worth? No matter what shape the money was in, no matter where it came from, it never decreased in value. It is the same with our worth to God; no matter where we came from, no matter what shape we show up in, we are priceless to God. Bank account balances and Facebook "likes" do not determine the worth of our lives. It does not matter who we are; it matters whose we are.

{A Warrior of Hope Knows Her Worth}

Perhaps you have struggled with feeling worthy or experienced great hurts by others who did not value you. But just as Jesus told the disciples, you are worth much to God, more than all other creation. He even knows the number of hairs on your head! Jesus wants you to know you are worth more than anything you can measure!

Heavenly Father, who knows the number of hairs on my head, thank you that you do not find my value in the same way the world does. Help me to get this God—I bear your image, Lord, and my circumstances do not change my value. Thank you for your steadfast love for me. In Jesus' name. Amen.

8.

Live Fiercely

Do not gloat over me, my enemy! Though I have fallen, I will rise. Though I sit in darkness, the Lord will be my light. Micah 7:8

There was a time once when I had to fight to keep what was mine. My job was in jeopardy, and I had a decision to make—leave or fight for my right to stay. This required me to stand up for myself and what I believed was right. It took courage to remain steadfast in my convictions and making the right decision depended on my determination to see the process through to the end.

Perhaps you too have had a time when you had to be fierce in the face of danger? Perhaps in your marriage, in your parenting, or in your career? If you have ever felt that passion rising within you because of a need to fight for what was right, you have lived fiercely.

Maybe you are fierce about a "cause." I volunteer in a Stop Human Trafficking ministry, and when I see injustice perpetrated against victims of sex or human trafficking, I become fierce in my stance against injustice.

A fierce woman derives her strength from a source beyond herself. Her identity is in Christ, forged through abiding in Him. Her commitment to God displays her courage, and her passion is not trivial. God wants to use these characteristics to fulfill His calling on our lives. We, like Esther (Esther 4:14), were made for such a time and calling as this. What stirs up this poignant, protective, powerful passion within you?

{A Warrior of Hope Lives Fiercely}

We may be broken or knocked down from time to time, and our enemies may think they have won, but they don't know the fierceness within the heart of a warrior. The light within us will radiate through the cracks and leave our enemy in the shadows. We will live fiercely!

Heavenly Father, I want to live fiercely for you. When life knocks me down, I will rise in your strength. When injustice is served, I will respond with fierce passion. Thank you for being the light that brightens my ways. Praise you for being my strength. In Jesus' name. Amen.

9.

He Lifted Me

He lifted me out of the slimy pit, out of the mud and mire; he set my feet on a rock and gave me a firm place to stand. Psalm 40:2

Have you ever wondered what the dirtiest job is? According to a recent Google search, it is a Garbage Collector. What's the messiest thing you have ever had to do?

When I was a teenager, we had horses. I loved riding and would spend many hours enjoying my horse and our long rides. However, the flip side of having a horse is taking care of them. The worst job of caring for horses is cleaning the stalls. There is no getting around it; we had to spend hours every week in the slimy stalls scooping out the muck and mire.

Sometimes in life, we feel like we have fallen into a pit of muck, mud, and mire. The feeling of hopelessness that follows that fall can seem overwhelming. The more we try to climb out of the slimy pit, the further we slide into overwhelming feelings of hopelessness.

I get it. I have battled addiction in the past, and the more I tried to resolve the issues with my own might, the dimmer my hope faded. It was when I cried out to the Lord and waited on Him, that transformation finally began. The Lord is faithful to pull us out of our slimy pits and place our feet on a rock, a firm place to stand, where the hope of healing and transformation will find us!

{A Warrior of Hope Stands On Firm Ground}

Are you in a pit? Do you want out? Friends, God loves us so much that sometimes He may allow us to fall into a pit, but He never leaves us there without a way out. His love may be difficult to understand sometimes, but He knows what we need to get back on the road to Him. If you are in a pit, ask for His help, He WILL lift you!

Heavenly Father, I know that you want to spend time with me and to have a deep relationship. I have fallen into a slimy pit and have forgotten your faithfulness for a time. Thank you for calling out to me to remind me you are here for me. I ask now for your help; I cannot do this on my own. I long to be lifted by you and to stand on firm ground. In Jesus' name. Amen.

10.

Confessions of A People Pleaser

Am I now trying to win the approval of human beings or God? Or am I trying to please people? If I were still trying to please people, I would not be a servant of Christ. Galatians 1:10

Who do you seek to please? Whose displeasure do you fear? Would you like to find freedom from this bondage?

I know these things about myself. 1.) I have a strong desire to please others. 2.) I look to others to tell me I am enough and worthy. 3.) No matter how hard I try to stop being a people pleaser, I am still one.

The truth is I've spent a good portion of my life waiting for other people to tell me I am ok. This crazy need to be recognized as worthy by the world has led to my people-pleasing behavior. So, how do we find the peace we crave and assurance of our worthiness?

The Word of God tells us we are fearfully and wonderfully made. We are seated in heavenly places with Christ. God has planned a future for us. We are precious in His eyes. We are His workmanship, and He exults over us with singing. With these kinds of accolades, why do we still seek the approval of men?

Friends, please hear me; this is not about following rules and changing our striving from pleasing people to pleasing God. No, this is about grace. This is about finding rest by trusting God. This is about a personal relationship with Jesus Christ.

{A Warrior of Hope Pleases the Lord}

No self-help book will help you find your worth. We have something better. We have the Gospel. We have a Father in Heaven who says we are worthy and we are enough. As we finish up today, turn to Psalm 139 and read what God thinks about you. God knows you, and He sees you. His hand is upon you.

Heavenly Father, I am exhausted from trying to please everyone, even you. I feel like anything I do is not enough. Please, Lord, help me to find rest in you and lean into this life of grace that you have created just for me. Thank you, Lord, you have a place for me and my mess, and you will never remove your hand from me. In Jesus' name. Amen.

11.

Motivational Mercies

The faithful love of the Lord never ends! His mercies never cease. Great is his faithfulness; his mercies begin afresh each morning. Lamentations 3:22-23 (NLT)

I love starting new things. I enjoy the energy that comes with a new project or endeavor. When we start on our new thing, it is easy to be encouraged and determined to see this new thing through to the end.

I recently started a 40-day sugar fast. The first two days were a breeze; I was walking around humming praises to the Lord and looking in the mirror, giving myself a wink with a "You got this girl" nod.

Then came the headaches. Not just slightly annoying headaches, but debilitating headaches, the ones you can't sleep through. My motivation started to slink out the back door.

So, how do we stay motivated? The truth is, we can't, at least not in our might. Motivation is an emotion, and emotions are fickle. I have identified three steps to staying motivated in my life, and I hope they are helpful to you also.

1. Be aware of when your motivation starts to slip. It usually happens about the same time Temptation rings the doorbell delivering Krispy Cream Donuts.
2. Turn to God. Start praying and recognize the strength we need to slam the door shut on Temptation only comes from God.
3. Be kind to yourself and show some gratitude. God is proud of you. It is ok to go back to that mirror and with a genuine smile, give God a nod and tell Him thanks for having your back, after all, that is what friends are for.

{A Warrior of Hope Is Motivated}

Let's forget all this self-help stuff and instead seek out a real encounter with the living God. This will help us to trust in the goodness and faithfulness of the Lord and rely on His motivational mercies that are never-ending.

Heavenly Father, great is your faithfulness, and I love that you grant me your mercies fresh every day! Forgive me for thinking I could do this without you! I love that you are my friend and have my back as I struggle with my goals. In Jesus' name. Amen.

12.

The Secret Place

But when you pray, go into your room, close the door and pray to your Father, who is unseen. Then your Father, who sees what is done in secret, will reward you. Matthew 6:6

Do you ever wonder if you are doing "prayer" right? Do you struggle with feeling the presence of God in your prayer time? Or question if He hears your prayers? Do you feel empty after prayer time, when you think you should feel satisfied?

When Jesus taught about prayer, His first lesson describes where we pray, not how we pray. He reveals the secret regarding where to pray in Matthew 6:6. He even provides instruction, a road map of sorts, for how to get there. 1.) Go into your room 2.) Shut the door. It does not have to be literal. Going into your room could be any place you can be alone. When we shut the door, we tune out all other distractions.

Here is the indispensable truth to the Secret Place; the Father is already there waiting for you. Look again at our verse, the Father walked into this space ahead of us, and His presence is already permeating the place. We have stepped onto Holy ground.

Sometimes we may have a prayer time that does not feel "holy" enough. Guess what? How you feel doesn't matter. Regardless of the lack of goosebumps or the sting of tears, you have stepped through His gates and stood on holy ground. We don't need a burning bush or a host of angels singing "Alleluia" to have an effective prayer life. We need to be obedient to God and walk into that Secret Place and pray.

{A Warrior of Hope Prays in Secret}

We can trust God that this practice of coming into the Secret Place will build intimacy with Him and create a firm foundation for our souls to stand on.

Heavenly Father, I open the door to my room and walk in to be greeted by your presence. I long for greater intimacy with you and a firm foundation for my soul to stand on. I know my prayer life is essential to a rewarding relationship with you. Thank you for providing me this Secret Place to pray. In Jesus' name. Amen.

13.

Unmovable Hope

If indeed you remain grounded and steadfast in the faith and are not shifted away from the hope of the gospel that you heard. Colossians 1:23a (CSB)

What is your "go-to" comfort in times of trouble? Do you often seek comfort in food, drink, or social media when you are stressed? I have used all of these as coping mechanisms in any given week. I may know better, but my life is a journey of many misconceptions, so I come from a place of grace when I say, let me try again.

In this letter from Paul to the Church at Colossae, he shows us we have everything we need in Christ. We have the hope of the gospel, the hope of eternal life, and the hope of unending joy. Yet, so often, I lose my way and let my feelings and emotions direct my feet through the kitchen on my way to the sofa, rather than turning to God for peace and my comfort.

Our inner peace is anchored to the immovable truths of God's Word. I am so thankful I have this assurance of the gospel, the gospel that guarantees my eternal life, and my joy. Despite what the people or circumstances are doing around me, I want to feel that my inner-soul peace, at my very core, is secure.

There is no sweeter message than the gospel, to know that no matter what your day has brought you, no matter how miserable or hopeless you "felt," you can go to bed at night with a quiet, peaceful heart. You can rest assured every sin you have ever committed or ever will commit is forgiven. This is the gospel truth.

{A Warrior of Hope is Steadfast}

God's Word is a steady assurance we can count on. Our hope is anchored in Christ Jesus. The world's teachings and ways are empty when compared to God's plan. We can reject shallow answers to our troubles and lean into the deep hope of our steadfast God.

Heavenly Father, I want to remain grounded and steadfast in my faith. I want to worship a God who is my real source of comfort. Take my hand and lead me to the rock of my salvation as I rest in your all-knowing wisdom. In Jesus' name. Amen.

14.

God Is Your Guide

Walk about Zion, go around her, count her towers, consider well her ramparts, view her citadels, that you may tell of them to the next generation. For this God is our God forever and ever; he will be our guide even to the end. Psalm 48:12-14

What is the most remote place you have ever visited? Did you have a guide with you? If you don't know the country or area you are traveling, it is wise to know your guide.

Once, when traveling in Mexico, we took a guided tour through some of the denser, forested areas of Mexico. The guide was able, because of his expertise, to show us things we would not have seen or noticed for ourselves. We saw and learned about Gum trees, hidden wildlife, and terrain specific to that area. Our guide also led us to a hidden gem in the middle of the forest, a beautiful waterfall and swimming hole. We were able to see a secret underwater cave we would never have seen without his knowledge and proficiency. How beautiful that excursion was and how grateful I was to have an expert guide to lead me!

A guide is essential in our daily living as well. We need both a map and a guide in our life as we maneuver through decisions and situations. It is important to know and trust your guides, as your safety is in their hands. We have the Word of God as our map and the Holy Spirit as our constant companion and our Guide. But if we fail to follow God's lead, we might miss out on some of the experiences He wants us to enjoy.

{A Warrior of Hope Follows God's Lead}

As we walk around the perimeter of our lives, inspecting the walls, counting our towers, and viewing our citadels (our hearts), let's make sure our foundation, our faith in God, remains strong. Let us then praise God for His protection and guidance.

Heavenly Father, you are my Guide and my God, forever and ever. There is no other in this world who can provide me with the wisdom and knowledge I need. I praise you for supplying me with your map and thank you for the Holy Spirit as my constant companion, even to the end. In Jesus' name. Amen.

15.

Unfading Beauty

Your beauty should not come from outward adornment, such as elaborate hairstyles and the wearing of gold jewelry or fine clothes. Rather, it should be that of your inner self, the unfading beauty of a gentle and quiet spirit, which is of great worth in God's sight. 1 Peter 3:3-4

Beauty treatments, facials, the cosmetic aisle at Target are all things I enjoy. How about you? What is your favorite pampering regimen? If you could change one thing about your physical appearance, what would it be?

When I was younger, I would mix Iodine and Baby Oil, smear it all over my body and layout by the pool for hours. I worshiped the sun and all its rays, begging it to make my skin a beautiful caramel brown. From time to time, I still crumple my face up in disdain at my "vampire" white coloring, but I no longer make that harmful mixture or try to change it. I now protect my white skin and go with what God gave me, grateful for the healthy state it is in.

Peter shares a vital truth with us in these verses. True beauty will reflect the love of God within you. Your attitude and your words will make the countenance of your face beautiful. God is not suggesting we have to be frumpy or dowdy to be good Christians; He is just letting us know, no matter how stunning our outward appearance is, it is the inner heart that brings about lasting beauty.

{A Warrior of Hope Has Unfading Beauty}

Be thankful for the body God has given you. Show it some love and gratitude by keeping it healthy. Then, after the creams, face masks and make-up have been removed, remember to do some "soul" care and soak in the rays of our Lord, whose *Son* shine will make all parts of you beautiful.

Heavenly Father, thank you for making my inner beauty of great worth and beauty in your sight. Help me to remember that what adorns my body is not as important as what adorns my heart. I want to have a quiet and gentle spirit that draws others to you through me. In Jesus' name. Amen.

16.

Rejoice in Suffering

Not only so, but we also glory in our sufferings, because we know that suffering produces perseverance; perseverance, character; and character, hope. And hope does not put us to shame, because God's love has been poured out into our hearts through the Holy Spirit, who has been given to us Romans 5:3-5

Are you surprised by suffering? How do you think we are to respond to suffering? Were you shocked to read in today's verse that we should respond to pain by rejoicing?

I recently had my writing critiqued. It was a situation where several writers got together and gave feedback on each other's writing. The feedback I received required me to re-write much of my essay. The feedback was painful and hard to hear, but after following through on her advice, I had improved. A little bit of suffering had produced an extraordinary outcome.

Our faith allows us to know what the world does not know; suffering produces an extraordinary outcome. It accomplishes something worthwhile. It presents three things that God wants to bless us with.

Through suffering, God increases our perseverance. It is like benching weights heavy enough to make our arms quiver and burn. By allowing ourselves to bear the burden, we end up stronger and steadier. God will develop your character to more closely resemble His Son's through your steadfastness. Others will recognize your strength and come to count on it; this makes you a more reliable person. Reliability produces hope. When people see how we have grown and changed to be more like Christ, they are encouraged to remain steadfast in their suffering.

{A Warrior of Hope Rejoices in Suffering}

If you are going through a time of suffering right now, I pray you will find the comfort you need in Christ. Take heart, this season of suffering will pass, and God will not waste any of your pain or tears. He is our Redeemer and uses everything according to His good purposes. He will use your new strength, perseverance, and character to bring hope to others you meet in your journey.

Heavenly Father, be with me in my time of suffering, be my hope for a better future. I pray to be able to hold steadfast under the weight of my situation, knowing you are here with me and will not let me fall. I pray for the character of Christ to shine through my cracks as I heal. In Jesus' name. Amen.

17.

Enough

Forget the former things; do not dwell on the past. See, I am doing a new thing! Now it springs up; do you not perceive it? I am making a way in the wilderness and streams in the wasteland. Isaiah 43:18-19

The enemy wants to keep us feeling the burden of shame and guilt. He hopes he can incapacitate you by continually filling your mind with your failings so that you won't try anything new again. What is one area in your life where you do not feel like you are enough? A place you lack confidence.

I did not make the team. It was devastating to hear I was not good enough and crushed to learn I did not get the position I had hoped for. It was debilitating to find out I could not participate in what I had longed to do.

It plays in my head like a reel of film that cannot be stopped, over and over again. "Not Good E*nough,*" starring me. It is the word "e*nough*" that catches me every time. You see, Satan is wise enough to know that long-term damage comes from crippling us, not killing us. I am good at this, just not good *enough*. I would have made the team if I had been just a little bit faster; I was just not fast *enough*. They loved me, but just not for this position. Not good *enough*.

It would be easy to give up and protect ourselves from getting hurt again by never trying, but it would be better if we could choose to tap into the power of Christ and rely on the strength of His Spirit in us. I wasn't strong enough, fast enough, resilient enough, or humble enough. But Christ in me was **more** than enough! And always will be.

{A Warrior of Hope Is Enough}

We can choose to turn our mind from everything *we are not* to everything we are….in the love of Christ. We can stop striving to be enough and rest in the assurance of all God has claimed us to be; loved, forgiven, worthy, lovely, and chosen. Enough.

Heavenly Father, today I choose to believe who you say I am, holy, loved, chosen, and worthy. I thank you that I am equipped by you, empowered by the Holy Spirit, and enveloped in Jesus Christ. You are my enough. In Jesus' name. Amen.

18.

Idle Words

Do not let any unwholesome talk come out of your mouths, but only what is helpful for building others up according to their needs. Ephesians 4:29

It was me. I was the one who gossiped about another person. Then the person I shared the gossip with, shared it with others, and they passed it on further still. I hurt so many people by speaking out of turn and sharing something that was not mine to share. I had sinned, and many paid the price for my sin.

The harm of gossip has affected everyone at some point in time. Whether the person meant to harm or not, the result of gossip is always broken trust and hurt feelings. God's Word warns us about speaking out of turn. We are to guard our mouths.

Would you gossip to God? There are things we would share with others, about others, but never say to God! But maybe there has been a time you have tried to glorify gossip? Found a way to have God endorse your sin? Or passed something off as a prayer request? Perhaps convinced yourself you are sharing this piece of information about the behavior or personal life of another for their benefit?

Sisters, if it does not pass the test of God's Word, stop and check your tongue. Are you whispering behind closed doors? Is this desire to share information in response to your insecurities? Do you have permission to share this information? Is it building the other person up? Would you say it to the face of the person you are talking about?

{A Warrior of Hope Builds Others Up}

I was able to apologize to the people I had hurt, and more importantly, I was able to apologize to God! Let's make a decision today to guard our tongues and be intentional about using our words to build others up.

Heavenly Father, I admit I am guilty of occasionally talking behind people's backs, and I am wrong for doing it. Please forgive my sin. Help me to be able to keep a tight rein on my words, so I don't hurt others. Show me ways to speak words that bring you glory and build others up. In Jesus' name. Amen.

19.

Don't Be a Fool

Let the wise listen and add to their learning, and let the discerning get guidance for understanding proverbs and parables, the sayings and riddles of the wise. The fear of the Lord is the beginning of knowledge, but fools despise wisdom and instruction. Proverbs 1:5-7

One of the most annoying types of people to be around is a know-it-all. The person who shares their opinion about everything but seldom listens or learns from others. Do you know anyone who fits that description?

I couldn't wedge a word into the conversation no matter how often I tried to interject. Every time I would start to say something, she would finish my sentence for me and rattle on about her opinion or experience. I finally gave up and just kept smiling and nodding, while in my head, I vowed to avoid talking to her again.

Solomon calls this type of person a fool. The fear of God is the beginning of knowledge because He is the Creator; all things have their origin in Him. By recognizing God as supreme and absolute, we can begin to see things as He does and have the discernment that guides us away from the foolish. But we can't do that if we're too busy running our own mouths to stop, listen, and learn from Him and others He has placed in our lives.

Once anchored in the fear of the Lord, we can continue the journey of learning. We can move beyond simple knowledge, knowing the facts, and proceed forward in wisdom, applying those facts to our lives.

{A Warrior of Hope Listens and Learns}

The book of Proverbs is filled with the sayings and riddles of the wise. We can learn how to apply this wisdom to daily life by listening and learning from this sage, old book. There are 31 chapters in the book of Proverbs, one for each day of the month. Don't just read these chapters, act upon them!

Heavenly Father, help me to be a wise person who adds to my learning and let discernment guide me. Thank you for the book of Proverbs and the wisdom I can find to help me in life. Fill me with your Spirit that I may never act foolishly. In Jesus' name. Amen.

20.

But God

My body and my mind may become weak, but God is my strength. He is mine forever. Psalm 73:26 (NCV)

Is weakness a gift? A gift of His grace? A gift that causes our knees to buckle and bow in surrender to God? Perhaps.

The word I was so tired of hearing hovered over my head until it hit my heart with a thud and instantly sank my spirit. "NO." Once again, I had tried to raise the banner of hope on my discouraging situation. I asked for approval for a procedure I knew could solve my problem. I wanted a "YES," but I got the dreaded "NO" instead. All my efforts to improve my situation had been met with defeat, leaving me feeling weak and weary.

But God. Often life hangs on those two words and what follows. The phrase "but God" appears hundreds of times in the Bible. One of my favorite, "But God" stories is Joseph and the coat of many colors. In this story, we see a boy whose life is not valued by his brothers and is sold into slavery. This story ends with one of the most famous "But God" statements: "You meant evil against me; *but* God meant it for good" (Genesis 50:20 NKJV).

No matter what proceeds the "but," God is your strength.

My body and mind are weak, **but God** is my strength. My problems are great, **but God** is my strength. My situation is exhausting, **but God** is my strength. My enemies surround me, **but God** is my strength. Whatever proceeds your "but", whatever your situation is, God is and always will be your strength.

{A Warrior of Hope Knows God's Strength}

The morning I received my "NO," I felt defeated, but only for a few minutes. God brought the verse above from Psalm 73:26 across my path within minutes of hearing a disappointing "NO." God's voice is so clear and His timing so perfect in reminding us no matter what our situation feels like, He is our strength.

Heavenly Father, it is in my weakness that you are strong. It is in the shadows of my mind that you are mighty. Thank you that no matter what proceeds my "but," you are God, and you are my strength forever. In Jesus' name. Amen.

21.

Spirit and Truth

But the time is coming—indeed it's here now—when true worshipers will worship the Father in spirit and in truth. The Father is looking for those who will worship him that way. John 4:23 (NLT)

As Warriors of Hope, we want to be the kind of worshipers the Father seeks, those who worship in spirit and truth. But how do we do that?

Poetry is a new form of worship I started practicing this past year. Either nature or Scripture inspires all the poems I write. Meditating on the beauty and truth of these two things causes my heart to respond to what has filled my mind. Both spirit and truth flow from that heart response out through my fingers and on to the paper in a mix of verses and stanzas.

Worship is defined as expressing praise and devotion. We often confuse worship as part of a ceremony, a church service. But it is also a lifestyle. God is Spirit; He is not limited to one place. He is present everywhere and can be worshiped anywhere, at any time.

We can bring worship into our daily lives in various ways:

by singing and dancing, keeping a gratitude journal, watching for everyday miracles, walking in nature, applauding God's creation, or by serving others. Worship is a way of life.

{A Warrior of Hope is a True Worshiper}

I want my life to be an offering of praise. I want to be a true worshiper with an attitude of gratitude, reverence, honor, and holy fear. How will you find ways to observe the Spirit of God in your day, and how will you respond as a true worshiper?

Heavenly Father, let me offer you a continual sacrifice of praise. Let me declare my devotion to you alone. Let my worship be genuine and true. I want my words to dance before you Lord in a symphony of praise. I never want to miss out on the miracles around me every day. May worship be my way of living. In Jesus' name. Amen.

22.

The Hard Question

For we do not have a high priest who is unable to empathize with our weaknesses, but we have one who has been tempted in every way, just as we are—yet he did not sin. Let us then approach God's throne of grace with confidence, so that we may receive mercy and find grace to help us in our time of need. Hebrews 4:15-16

When are you most aware of God's grace and mercy? Is it when you are thriving, and life is going well? Or is it when you are needy and feeling challenged?

Asking for help is hard. I typically prefer to try to do it on my own, over and over again. Eventually, tears of frustration and a few dramatic gestures finally deflate my rebellion and cause me to look up. God wants us to ask Him the hard question: "Can you help me?"

It is clear, from the beginning of time, that God created us to need His help. God's provision for us from creation—food, water, and companionship—shows us we were created to need Him. But God also created us as helpers, beginning with Eve, showing us His desire for us to help one another. "It is not good for man to be alone. I will make a helper suitable for him" (Genesis 2:18).

This means our need for help is not a sign of failure or a reason for shame. God created us to need help. We have a Savior who empathizes with our needs and understands our weaknesses. He is reaching out His hand to us, so we may receive mercy and find grace to help in our time of need.

{A Warrior of Hope Confidently Asks for Help}

We also can help others. We can pick them up when they are weak and show them the way to God's throne of grace. We have all been in a place of frailty and needed a helping hand. Go ahead and ask the hard question. You were created to give and receive help!

Heavenly Father, give me the confidence to approach your throne of grace and ask for your mercy. Help me to be a good helpmate to others as well, never allowing pride to keep me from admitting my need for help. In Jesus' name. Amen.

23.

A Good Laugh

Sarah said, "God has brought me laughter, and everyone who hears about this will laugh with me." Genesis 21:6

I love a good laugh, and I bet you do too. Who in your life always makes you laugh? Has God ever made you laugh?

I love the story of Abraham and Sarah. It is filled with the kind of laughter that comes from a place of pure joy and fulfilled hope. It starts when God tells Abraham he is going to be a Dad. "Abraham fell facedown; he laughed and said to himself, "Will a son be born to a man a hundred years old? Will Sarah bear a child at the age of ninety?" (Genesis 17:17) I can see the humor in this, can't you?

Later, with a newborn son in her arms, Sarah understood the goodness of a God who keeps His promises, and she laughed. Maybe it was that adrenaline let down we sometimes experience at the end of a stressful situation, like childbirth (no epidurals back then!). Or perhaps she understood God was laughing with her, so she laughed and urged others to laugh too, not because the situation was ridiculous, but because it was wondrous. Guess what they named their son? Isaac, which means "laughter."

The story of Abraham and Sarah is brimming with laughter

and the goodness of God. He truly desires to bless us with the desires of our hearts. I can imagine God gets a good chuckle from time to time when He blesses us.

{A Warrior of Hope is Filled with Laughter}

We are reminded there is a time for everything, "a time to weep and a time to laugh." (Ecclesiastes 3:4) I am thankful laughter is part of my relationship with God. What is one thing God has done in your life that made you laugh?

Heavenly Father, I am glad that laughter is part of our life together. Help me never to take myself too seriously so that I can enjoy a good laugh when I need to. Your goodness to me has brought me much joy, thank you! In Jesus' name. Amen.

24.

What We Really Need

Then the Lord said to Moses, "I will rain down bread from heaven for you. The people are to go out each day and gather enough for that day.
Exodus 16:4a

Have you ever wished away your contentment? What I mean is, have you ever convinced yourself that what you currently have is not good enough?

A recent trip to Hobby Lobby made me acutely aware of how easy I can wish away my contentment. I left home completely satisfied with my kitchen décor. After perusing the aisles of farmhouse décor, I had filled my cart with cotton wreaths and whitewashed signs that I *NEEDED* to be happy with my kitchen again. Sometimes what I have or the things I want don't line up with what God gives me.

The story of the Israelites in the wilderness paints such a beautiful picture of God's provision for His people. God's miraculous distribution of food, not too much or too little, is an illustration of the Lord's grace and generosity. God gave food to the people regardless of their attitudes or beliefs

The manna from heaven wasn't what the Israelites wanted, but it was what they needed. Even though they grumbled and asked for meat, God continued to provide for them. So often we become foolish in our desires, believing what we have is not good enough or thinking something as trivial as farmhouse décor can fill a genuine need within us. When the truth is, God knows precisely what we need, and He is faithful to provide it for us.

{A Warrior of Hope Appreciates God's Provision}

I have come to realize I have chosen to be dissatisfied with trivial things such as home décor, instead of content with the beauty of God's provision all around me. My heart's desire is to look at what I have with fresh eyes and be content with the miracle of manna and not wish away God's grace and generosity. How about you? Are you able to see God's miraculous provision in your life?

Heavenly Father, thank you for your provisions. I am sorry for the times I grumble about what I have. I want to live a life of contentment and gratitude. Help me to see the beauty in your grace and generosity that falls fresh around me every morning. In Jesus' name. Amen.

25.

A Song in my Heart

The LORD your God, is with you, the Mighty Warrior who saves. He will take great delight in you; in his love he will no longer rebuke you but will rejoice over you, with singing. Zephaniah 3:17

Have you ever questioned whether or not you were worthy of God's love? I have.

I had failed to be a good Christian. My mind was troubled because I did not act "Christian" enough at the event. I had a good time and never once mentioned Jesus or my faith in the evening of conversation. I couldn't help but imagine God's disappointment in me.

So often we feel like we have to earn God's love by not messing up or by doing great things. We make our imaginary lists of what is considered good, appropriate, or worthy of God's approval. When we miss the mark, we stand back from God and fret about it.

But, only after I realized I could never earn His love could I rejoice in the knowledge that I don't have to. God, along with all of heaven, rejoices over each of us who receives His gift of faith.

No matter what you've done or failed to do, you are not a

failure in His eyes. He is glad that you are His. He rejoices over you with singing. There is nothing in this world you could have done differently to stop His love for you. God created you to be with Him, to be known by Him, and to be rejoiced over by Him.

{A Warrior of Hope is a Delight to the Lord}

Find the courage, my friend, in the fact that you are a child of the Mighty Warrior who saves, and Who rejoices over you with singing.

Heavenly Father, thank you for the hope that comes from knowing you. I exalt your name while I sit in your presence and soak in your loving touch as you sing over me. In Jesus' name. Amen

26.

Think Before You Speak

My dear brothers and sisters, take note of this: Everyone should be quick to listen, slow to speak and slow to become angry. James 1:19

Are you a good listener? How about being a great speaker? Does the information you read, see, or hear in the news today ever elicit an angry reaction? The simple passage in James written 2000 years ago is as difficult to put into action today as it was then.

A recent Google search revealed that, on average, we send 2.4 million emails, 6000 Tweets, and over 300,000 texts **per second**. We are receiving information live 24/7/365, and we listen without hearing, speak without thinking, and react without filtering.

Wisdom begins when we listen more and talk less. The Word of God is more available to us now than ever before, yet I wonder if we can even hear it over the constant noise of life? The older I get, the more I realize I've never been as wise as I thought I was. And my instinctual responses to perceived wrongs are rarely right. I've learned to slow down, wait, and think about my responses with a clear head before firing off a defensive retort in all caps. I am thinking before speaking.

James was not saying; "don't get angry." He is saying to be slow to become angry. The type of anger we should avoid is a deep-rooted outrage that bubbles up in us than explodes all over everyone around us. It is messy anger expelled without control. When we are slow to anger, we exercise control over our emotions and extend grace to others as God has given to us. Where sin is multiplied, grace is multiplied more.

{A Warrior of Hope is Quick to Listen and Slow to Speak}

The human heart endures the same condition it did when we started. There is nothing new under the sun. The precepts written on scrolls 2000 years ago hold the same truth we read today, whether in a scroll, in a Bible or on the internet. The more we learn from these precepts, the more likely we become to extend grace instead of hate.

Heavenly Father, your precepts from 2000 years ago continue to hold such valuable truths for me today. I yearn to learn all that you have to teach me. Help me in my efforts to tame my tongue and offer value to others in what I speak, both written and spoken. In Jesus' name. Amen.

27.

Good Gifts

Which of you, if your son asks for bread, will give him a stone? Or if he asks for a fish, will give him a snake? If you, then, though you are evil, know how to give good gifts to your children, how much more will your Father in heaven give good gifts to those who ask him! Matthew 7:9-11

What is the best gift you have ever received? How about one you hated? Perhaps you have received a "gag" gift at some point in time? Let's look at the gifts God wants us to have.

The worst gift I ever received was a pair of cherry-red, corduroy, bell-bottom pants. I had wanted a pair of bell-bottom pants for Christmas and was hopeful I would go back to school in January sporting those trendy white "hot pants" that were all the rage.

If your son asks for bread, will you give him a stone? We, even in our sinful nature, are not likely to withhold a truly good gift from our children. However, sometimes, the gifts God gives us do not look like what we expect in this life. God's ways are higher than our ways, and His thoughts greater than our thoughts. As hard as it can be to let go of what I thought I wanted, the realization that God's wisdom is beyond my comprehension helps me to trust that He knows what's best.

God graciously guides us in understanding what the Word has to offer is far superior to what the world has to offer. The gift He so desires for us to unwrap is more of His Word, His wisdom, His ways, more of Him.

{A Warrior of Hope Receives Good Gifts}

The absence of trendy white hot pants under the Christmas tree that year, although it felt like a stone to my heart, was probably a beautiful gift from a parent whose ways and thoughts were higher than mine. God does not always provide for us in the ways we might expect in this life, but I am OK with that, knowing He always has my best interests in mind! Are you?

Heavenly Father, you have given me such beautiful gifts. Your ways are superior to mine and your blessings more generous than any gift the world can offer me. I am grateful for the gift of my salvation, which gives me an eternity with my Father in heaven. Forgive me for the times I have not been grateful or content with your generosity. In Jesus' name. Amen.

28.

I Pinky Swear

Through these he has given us his very great and precious promises, so that through them you may participate in the divine nature, having escaped the corruption in the world caused by evil desires.
2 Peter 1:4

Have you ever broken a promise? Perhaps you have had someone break their promise to you? How does it feel when we can't rely on someone's word? Does it make you less likely to trust them in the future?

We were a group of four or five girls who met in the hollowed-out part of the bush lined fence on the playground. We huddled together and created a secret club. I have long forgotten what we called our club, but I do remember all of us linking our pinky fingers together and swearing never to tell anyone about our secret club. We may only have been kids, but even then we knew the importance of a promise.

God's monumental, significant, and enduring promises are no secret. His precious and reliable promises are all spelled out for us in His Word. We don't have to be part of a hidden club to receive them, and we can rely on Him to never break them. In the span of 4000 years (from Abraham to now) the Lord's promises have held true, they are His infallible pledge to us.

How do we know we can rely on God's promises? In Numbers 23:19, we read this truth: "God is not human, that he should lie, not a human being, that he should change his mind. Does he speak and then not act? Does he promise and not fulfill?" God is not capable of breaking a promise; it is not part of His divine nature.

{A Warrior of Hope Relies on God's Promises}

As Warriors of Hope, we rely on God's promises and partake of His divine nature. Simply put, through our salvation, we received a new nature that will not perish but will live on into eternity with our Promise Maker, Promise Keeper.

Heavenly Father, thank you for your promises. Help me to learn each of them by spending time in your Word. Thank you for rescuing me from the corruption of this world through salvation and for the privilege of participating in your divine nature. In Jesus' name. Amen.

29.

Restored

And the God of all grace, who called you to his eternal glory in Christ, after you have suffered a little while, will himself restore you and make you strong, firm and steadfast. 1 Peter 5:10

Have you seen the home improvement shows where there are before and after pictures? Or shows where people repurpose old furniture into more attractive, useful pieces? There is something appealing about seeing something old and drab restored to something beautiful, isn't there?

I believe each of us has areas where restoration is necessary. Rooms in our heart where past hurts have left us damaged. Old belief systems that need to be stripped away and replaced with truths. Drab and worn-out habits that do not work for us anymore. Or maybe you need a physical restoration?

Peter is writing this letter to bring encouragement to suffering Christians. We too need to hear these words of encouragement before we suffer from obliterating hope and give in to the temptation of giving up. As Warriors of Hope, we can look at how God is bringing restoration to our lives and share this hope with others.

Peter was able to give us a wider perspective on our pain

and suffering. In comparison to eternity, our suffering will last only "a little while" before God will restore us and make us strong, firm, and steadfast. Some of us will be delivered from our pain in this lifetime, and some of us will be restored and see relief from suffering through death.

{A Warrior of Hope Lives Restored}

My favorite picture of eternity is this: imagine one single drop of water added to a very large bucket of water. That single drop of water represents the amount of time we spend on earth. The rest of the water in the bucket, in the pond, in the lake, in the ocean…represents eternity. Be encouraged by Peter's words that "a little while" is nothing compared to eternity.

Heavenly Father I am so grateful for a God who intends to restore my old, drab parts to perfection. I look forward to the healing and restoration that will come to me, both in my time on earth and the suffering I will be released from through death. Thank you for the promise of an eternity spent with you. In Jesus' name. Amen.

30.

Our Final Hope

The foundations of the city walls were decorated with every kind of precious stone. The first foundation was jasper, the second sapphire, the third agate, the fourth emerald, the fifth onyx, the sixth ruby, the seventh chrysolite, the eighth beryl, the ninth topaz, the tenth turquoise, the eleventh jacinth, and the twelfth amethyst. The twelve gates were twelve pearls, each gate made of a single pearl. The great street of the city was of gold, as pure as transparent glass. Revelation 21:19-21

What is your wildest dream? If you could go anywhere in the world, where would you travel? I am enamored with the fact there is a whole other world underwater in our oceans. If I could go anywhere, it would be to the bottom of the ocean!

My husband and two boys are obsessed with superheroes. They watch all the TV Shows about them and go to every movie involving the stories of their imaginary heroes. I don't know if the fascination stems from their superpowers, the imaginary worlds where they often live, or if it is simply the power of a good plot. But they thoroughly enjoy these stories, and I can't blame them.

I, too, love a good fantasy, a wild dream, a reason to hope for a better reality than what I am currently experiencing. As I read the book of Revelation, I feel like I am reading a fantasy novel. God's extravagant provision described in the verses above, seems almost fantastical, perhaps because the scope of God's creativity is unimaginable to me.

But what is not fantasy is God's Word. If our future is not secured and satisfied in the Lord, we will forever be hopeless. Our souls will wither and die. Our throats will remain parched. Our insides will cringe with pain. Our hearts will cry out into the wilderness and receive no response.

{A Warrior of Hope has the Gift of Eternal Life}

If you have come this far and do not know, without question, that you belong to and are forever loved by the God of all creation, the Maker of the heavens and earth, the Lord of all the universe, please join me in this prayer to receive salvation and eternal life.

Heavenly Father, I know that I am a sinner, and ask for your forgiveness. I believe you died for my sins and rose from the dead. By faith, I invite you into my heart and receive you as my Lord and Savior. Thank you for the gift of eternal life. In Jesus' name. Amen.

31.

A Quiver of Arrows

He made my mouth like a sharpened sword, in the shadow of his hand he hid me; he made me into a polished arrow and concealed me in his quiver.
Isaiah 49:2

As we come to the end of our 30 days together, I want to leave you with some tools for the future. As we have explored the Word of God and connected with the Ultimate Warrior of Hope Himself, our King, we become anchored in the hope of Jesus Christ. You don't have to face tomorrow's battles empty-handed or defenseless. The Lord has indeed made you into a polished arrow and carries you Himself in His very own quiver!

You are a warrior. A Warrior of Hope. You are stronger than your past and mightier than the challenges in your future. Your scars are your battle cry. Wear them proudly and be thankful for the way God uses the pain in your life to make you stronger.

You are more than a survivor; you are a warrior. A Warrior of Hope. When you fall, you get up and stand taller and walk with even greater confidence. Jesus has made you His warrior to keep hope alive. You are not meant to remain concealed in His quiver, but to be used as a Warrior of

Hope, spreading His light and His love to the world around you.

{A Warrior of Hope Knows Her Purpose...

To Release Hope into the World!}

God has called and equipped you to release His hope into the world. It's time to move this battle forward. Nothing is going to stop you; you have God's faith as your shield and His strength inside you to fight. You are the arrow of hope!

Heavenly Father, I respond to your call on my life to be a Warrior of Hope and thank you that you have equipped me with everything I need to be your vessel of hope to a hurting world. Thank you for my past, which makes me stronger and more confident in my future. In Jesus' name. Amen.

The Warrior of Hope Manifesto

- A Warrior of Hope Gets What She Prays For
- A Warrior of Hope Lets the Lord Lead the Way
- A Warrior of Hope Receives Her Strength from the Lord
- A Warrior of Hope Lives Inspired
- A Warrior of Hope Trusts God's Timing
- A Warrior of Hope Has Faith
- A Warrior of Hope Knows Her Worth
- A Warrior of Hope Lives Fiercely
- A Warrior of Hope Stands on Firm Ground
- A Warrior of Hope Pleases the Lord
- A Warrior of Hope is Motivated
- A Warrior of Hope Prays in Secret
- A Warrior of Hope is Steadfast
- A Warrior of Hope Follows God's Lead
- A Warrior of Hope has Unfading Beauty
- A Warrior of Hope Rejoices in Suffering
- A Warrior of Hope is Enough
- A Warrior of Hope Builds Others Up
- A Warrior of Hope Listens and Learns
- A Warrior of Hope Knows God's Strength

- A Warrior of Hope is a True Worshiper
- A Warrior of Hope Confidently Asks for Help
- A Warrior of Hope is Filled with Laughter
- A Warrior of Hope Appreciates God's Provision
- A Warrior of Hope is a Delight to the Lord
- A Warrior of Hope is Quick to Listen and Slow to Speak
- A Warrior of Hope Receives Good Gifts
- A Warrior of Hope Relies on God's Promises
- A Warrior of Hope Lives Restored
- A Warrior of Hope has the Gift of Eternal Life
- A Warrior of Hope Knows Her Purpose…to Release Hope into the World!

Closing Thoughts

I pray as you have read through these devotions, you have become anchored in the hope we have in Christ Jesus, and you are overflowing with joy and peace. It has been an honor to connect with each of you as we become Warriors of Hope!

If you joined me in the Sinner's Prayer on Day 30, please know that not only am I rejoicing, but the angels are rejoicing, and the Holy Spirit of the Living God is now in you. If we never meet here on earth, I look forward to celebrating with you in heaven!

Most assuredly, I say to you, he who hears My word and believes in Him who sent Me has everlasting life, and shall not come into judgment, but has passed from death into life. John 5:24(NKJV)

About the Author

Laurie Hampton is a devoted follower of Jesus Christ, wife, mother, writer, and blogger. She founded the ministry, Beautifully Broken, to encourage, inspire, and point people to Jesus. You can connect with her at www.lauriehampton.com.

Laurie has always loved learning about Jesus and studying His Word. As a child, she attended elementary school at Our Savior's Lutheran School, where she fell in love with Jesus and sharing His love with everyone around her. She holds a Writing Certificate from Maple Woods Community College and has been active in her local writing guild.

Laurie's other creative interests include writing essays and poetry, blogging, quilting and scrapbooking. She lives in the beautiful state of Missouri with her husband and near her two adult children.

I'd love to hear from you!

To write to me personally or to get connected to my weekly devotions, visit my website at www.lauriehampton.com

www.ingramcontent.com/pod-product-compliance
Lightning Source LLC
Chambersburg PA
CBHW031309060426
42444CB00033B/1148